RIDE THE WAVE

Your Relationship with Grief

Zipporiah S. Brockman

Holbrook||**Publishing**

Ride The Wave. Copyright © 2023 by Zipporiah S. Brockman. All rights reserved. Printed in the United States of America. No part of this book may be used or reproduced in any manner whatsoever without written permission,

except in the case of brief quotations embodied in critical articles and reviews. For information address Holbrook Publishing, Jacksonville, AR 72076

Holbrook Publishing books may be purchased for educational, business, or sales promotional use. For information please email: holbrookpublishing@aol.com

Cover *Designed by: Zipporiah S.Brockman*

Library of Congress Cataloging-in-Publication Data has been applied for. ISBN 9798882677854

Table of Content

Introduction

Chapter 1: The Tragedy: Initial Shock

Chapter 2: What Do I Feel?

Chapter 3: Even if You Prepare, You're Not Prepared

Chapter 4: Feel What You Feel, No Apologies.

"Don't tell me how to grieve"

Chapter 5: Do Not Compare "We are not the same"

Dearly Beloved: The Cost of Love

This book is dedicated to every Survivor.

"So, in the end, she won. Every experience lifted her. Every tragedy taught her that survival renders painful victories sorted throughout time. She relaxed knowing that once she survived one day, she could survive a thousand more."

Zipporiah

Introduction

I Call Bull Shhh!!! That's about all I could say the moment I got the call that my brother had been shot. I couldn't and wouldn't believe it, but my gut told me to rush to his home anyway. I left my mom (not on purpose) and drove frantically to his home. When I turned onto his street, I saw the ambulance and fire trucks. I saw tons of people standing around and one officer (who was a friend of ours) with tears in his eyes. He said," Zippy, it doesn't look good. Get to the hospital." I immediately jumped back in my truck and headed to the hospital. My mom, grandmother and other family members started to gather at the hospital. I saw them bring my brother inside and the look of peace on his face made me feel better. It was just 10 minutes later when they called my family to the back. My mother kept saying, "If he was okay they wouldn't call us back here. The doctor came back, and I will never unhear his words. They cut a hole in my heart that will never go away. My entire world changed on May 24,2011.

The next thing I had to do was call my older brother and tell him that Michal was dead. I will never forget that day and the days of tragedy that seemed to follow. The one thing that stuck out to me in all the death that has occurred in my family is people steering our grief. People who may or may not know they are hindering or hurting the process by forcing traditional and often "religious rhetoric" down our throats to either make us feel better or grieve faster. I've started to believe it is the latter. My experience with death in my immediate family changed everyone's life. I grew up with my brother's, my mom and grandmother all under the same roof. From children to adults, even if we moved out, that was home. After Michal was killed, my grandmother was diagnosed with Liver Cancer and only given a few months to live. She died on

January 7, 2013. Six months later we were getting ready to leave home headed to a conference where my mom had to minister. As we were getting dressed, my mom and I saw a State Trooper entering the driveway. We both laughed thinking, "What did Awkii do now?" The officer knocked on the door and from the look on his face we knew it was much more serious. That's when he explained that Awkii had been killed in a single car accident early that morning. My mother just sat down crying; I was so upset I punched a hole in the wall. My task then was telling my dad that Awkii was dead. It was the weekend so we couldn't see him to identify his body. My dad was in denial until we confirmed it was him. Losing my oldest brother was another blow to my heart I wasn't ready to handle.

A few years later, February 2, 2016, I was in a meeting when I was told to get to the hospital to see about my mother. When I got there, I learned that she had suffered a heart attack and stroke. I was told that she died but they worked tirelessly to get her back after 6 minutes. Thankfully my mother is still here, but that stroke left her speech botchy, physically unable to do some things and with a brain injury that affected her sight. The following year on June 17, 2017, my grandfather passed away after battling Alzheimer's. It broke my heart not knowing how sick he was and the day I was going to visit, I got the call that he died.

You would think I was done but a year later, September 23, 2018, I and a few other friends were scheduled to meet up at my god sister/best friend's home. I had been calling her all day but never got and answer. Later that night I got the call that she was found dead in her apartment. Cheryl and I literally talked every single day. She understood my obsession with cheese and the quirky things that made me laugh. With so much transition in my life, one would think I am an expert on grief but I'm not. After almost 9 years since my brother Michal passed, I am just now getting to the place that I recognize and understand where things went wrong for me. I never grieved their deaths. I never made "feeling" a priority and it wasn't until I started reading comments on Facebook of people whose loved ones died that I realized what happened to me. I hope that in this book you will take the time to understand what you feel and know that it is okay to put your emotions first. No matter your position in that person's life. It is not your job to place anyone's grief above your own. My desire is that each person who reads this book will learn their own process and be able to prioritize their emotions without fear or worry that they may be "doing too much" or taking too long. There is no time limit on grief.

Chapter 1

The Tragedy: Initial Shock

First things first. Let's define death.

Death-

Noun

The action or fact of dying or being killed, the end of life the life of a person or organism.

We of course know what death is. Everyone has had to experience the death of someone and as it's always been told, "We all have to go that way at some point." When you initially experience the death of your loved one, emotionally some are all over the place trying to scramble to find anything that will settle the severe anxiety that they are dealing with. Then there are those who go numb. Those are the people who seemingly act as if nothing has happened. They behave almost identical to those who are in denial. That first pain is one I don't think anyone can ever forget. It's that lump in your throat and the pain in your heart that feels just as real as someone hitting you in the face with a brick. In all honesty, I really can't describe it, but it is unforgettable. There are things that happen and things that are said when someone dies that you never forget. For me, it was when my brother Michal was killed. That day will forever be etched in my brain. I remember where I was and exactly what I was doing when my mom walked in and told me Michal had been shot. Not thinking about her or anyone else, I jumped in my truck and rushed to his home.

I remember the ambulance, fire trucks and all the people seemingly staring at me. I remember being told by a cop to get to the hospital, so I got in my truck and drove to the hospital. I remember the EMT pulling up and bringing him inside. He had the most peaceful look on his face, and I thought, "He's going to be okay!"

When my mother and grandmother got there, I was smiling because he was okay. I knew he was okay. They called our family to the back. I remember it was just me, my mom, my grandmother and my brother's friend Byron. My brother Awkii refused to come because that's just how he was. He hated hospitals. I remember the doctor walking in, he was super short. His words I will never forget. "The hardest part of my job is to tell a family that their loved one is deceased." I screamed and ran out of the hospital and collapsed in the parking lot. I couldn't breathe, I couldn't hear, I couldn't see, I couldn't talk. Everything was still.

The Sun was beaming on my back, tears rolling down my face and all I could think was this is not real. I felt someone tugging on my shirt and when I looked back it was a nurse. She was trying to get me off the ground. When I stood up, I was pacing frantically looking for my mom and my grandmother. It was like they just disappeared. By that time phone calls had started coming from family members, text messages and Facebook post. Everything from that day is so vivid. I found my grandmother sitting in the waiting room with her head down. I couldn't find my mom, but she had gone down the street to get Sandra, Michal's ex-wife/best friend.

The nurse came out and asked if we wanted to see him and of course we did. If you knew the relationship I had with my brothers, especially Michal you would probably find this next part funny. The nurse directed us to the room they had him in. My mom was in front with Sandra, and I was holding my grandmother's hand. As soon as we hit the corner and granny saw Michal she screamed," Lawd my baby" and hit the floor. It was one of the saddest moments in my life, but I could only laugh hearing Michal saying," Now Dammit Granny, you can't just fall out like that!" I'm not an expert on grief but I do know that in that moment none of what I saw was real to me. In that moment something locked in my head that Michal was just on vacation and that he would be back.

It wasn't anything I just sat and thought about, it literally just clicked and stayed there. From that exact moment, everything I did was almost robotic. I was given the task to plan Michal's funeral. My mom, dad and brother knew Michal and I were soul mates. My mom always said we were two bodies with one heart. He was my best friend, my chef, my comedian and him and Awkii let me dress them up with clothes from granny's closet. That was always a good laugh.

In the days before the funeral our family stood together, but in the months to come, we could see how death changed the dynamics of our family. Everyone seemed to be in a zone. It was like we all were just existing at this point. We weren't as eager to be around each other, and my mom kept herself super busy. I tried to be as normal as I could, but things were not the same. I didn't really know how to laugh anymore. Nothing was funny. Nobody could get the laugh out of me that Mike could, but I was still holding on to the fact that he would be back from his vacation pretty soon. Our family home changed.

There seemed to be a presence, a scent, a looming love that had departed.

Death changed our family and when he came, he came quickly once again. It's crazy that I never knew how sick my grandmother was. I knew she had a surgery some years ago on her liver to remove something, but I never knew what that "something" was. Later that year mom said it was cancer. I was a little upset with my grandmother because she didn't really keep secrets from me. She told me everything, even stuff I didn't want to know. I can remember the visit to UAMS hospital. My mother and grandmother went back for the results of a test. Mom came out walking fast with tears in her eyes. Before I could ask her why she was crying she just said, "I am going to get the car!" I leaned over and asked granny what they said, and she told me, "They said to go home. There is nothing else they can do." I looked at my granny and said," Well we bout to kick it then!" She laughed and we took a picture right there laughing. For my mother, it was a devastating day.

For my granny and I it was Game On! They gave her 3 weeks that October, but she lived to see her 88th birthday on December 07,2012. I asked her to promise me that she would dance with me on my birthday and on December 31,2012 she stood, weak and frail, but she danced with me. On January 7th, 2013, at 7:33 AM my sweet girl made her transition.

It was hard to watch my mother weep as much as she did when her mother died. My mom is the only girl, and my grandmother spoiled her rotten. Everything changed when the Matriarch passed away. I think myself; my mother and my brother Awkii were in a daze. Granny basically raised us when our parents got divorced. When mom moved, granny insisted that we stay with her until my mom got on her feet. Her home was always open, so no matter where we went and how long we stayed away, we knew we could always come back to granny. My granny raised us, but Awkii was her baby.

I knew that when she left, Awkii would take it hard because she was his everything. She always protected him and that was something he could count on. Awkii started drinking more than usual after she died. He and his then girl friend had broken up and she left with his son. He had expressed to me that he felt like everything had been taken from him. One day he came to granny's house and was clearly drunk, but it seemed as though he had taken something because he was different. He came inside and intentionally picked a fight with my mom. In his anger and our arguing, he drove his hand through the window. Covered in blood, he stood there crying that Michal and granny were dead and he blamed my mother.

I knew she wasn't the cause and so did he, but I knew all of what he felt and the hurt he never expressed came to the surface. After that incident, he needed to cool off so he went to stay with my grandparents for a few days. Things got better from there for him. He rekindled his relationship with his youngest son's mom and moved to the country. He was in a very good place. I remember he called my mom on her birthday, and they spent most of the call laughing. I spoke with him via text the next day. He just said, "Love you Nae" I responded with," Love you too Ke".

It was in the early morning of July 20,2013. Mom was supposed to sing at a conference in Little Rock. We were getting dressed when we saw a state trooper and local officer vehicles coming down the driveway. I called mom to the living room saying," What in the world did

Awkii do now?!" We met the officer at the door and by the look on his face I knew something was wrong. He told us that Awkii had been killed in a single car accident early that morning. The officer had to catch my mom, I ran down the hall and punched the wall as hard as I could. This had to be a joke. It wasn't real to me. I took a deep breath and grabbed my phone to call my dad. Just as I was, my father was in shock and didn't believe it was him. We had to wait all until Monday morning to visit the mortuary and identify my brother's body. The pain in my heart, nobody could measure. I was angry, hurt and a little relieved at the same time. You may ask, "Why were you relieved?" My brother was always a target. He had friends who betrayed him. There were times when I felt the cops were out to get him. He just seemed to attract danger. Awkii was not without his fair share of trouble making, but he was a good man with a gentle heart. Nobody can ever take that away from him. I was very broken that he was gone, but relieved because I knew he was safe.

What's your story?

Chapter 2

How Do I Feel?

You've just lost your loved one. The first question everyone asks is," How do you feel?" Right now, you may be numb, you may seem normal, or you may be an emotional mess. This is not the time to try to explain how you feel in depth, but if you can, talk to someone who can listen without inserting. This is fresh and you don't really know. It's a confusing place, a fearful place, sometimes a dark place filled with all sorts of emotions and feelings. You don't really know what to do, what to think, how to think or even act. If you're too normal some will think you don't care. If you're too emotional then some will think you're being dramatic. At the end of the day, no matter the level of the loss, you are entitled to feel, think or act in any way that is safe and okay for you. What anyone thinks is not your concern. At least it shouldn't be. There is no textbook way to do things when it comes to grief. In all actuality you don't really start grieving immediately.

One of the most amazing things I ever witnessed was the day the cops showed up to tell us that my oldest brother had been killed in a car wreck. My mother instantly broke down. She was scheduled to sing at a conference later that morning. After the notification, I asked her if I needed to call and cancel. She said, "No! I must complete this assignment." I was in complete shock, but as her drummer and a true believer of the God in her, I packed up my stuff and we went to church. I know that although she did what she did because of her relationship with God, she was also operating on adrenaline. Afterwards, she wanted to visit people and behaved as if nothing had ever happened. I was broken inside, but I felt like I had to have the same energy my mother had to not take away from the fact that she had just lost another child. There were 3 of us and now it was just me. I didn't think about my feelings at the time. I could only focus on my mother. We had just buried my grandmother (her mother) 6 months ago and my baby brother a year before that. To me, there was no room for what I was feeling at the time. At least that's what I thought. I had no idea that my way of thinking and processing would ultimately cause me so much emotional harm years later. How do I feel? I still can't really explain it, but some days I am okay and other days I want to cry all day. I get angry. I battle depression and honestly, I have had suicidal ideation. You will go through an array of emotions, but in the beginning, you don't know and it's okay to say that. It's okay to not answer. Don't tell people, "I'm okay" or "I'll be fine". I say that because you'll start saying it so much that you talk yourself into believing that "right away" you will be those things. If you have a higher power just advise them to pray for you or send positive energy your way. Pretending to be okay only sets you up for emotional blockage. It may sound like a harsh thing to say, but you are responsible for your emotions. How you handle what you feel during the initial phase of grief has to be your priority. Expecting anyone to understand is doing yourself a disservice. How you feel should be just as much a priority as anyone else.

How do you feel?

Chapter 3

Even if You Prepare, You're Not Prepared.

When someone passes away suddenly, we all feel as though things are left unsaid, undone. You don't get the opportunity to say goodbye. One could also say that the pain is far worse than it is when you've been told that your loved one has only a certain amount of time to live. In my opinion, when you have that closure it doesn't lessen the pain, but it helps with the process. When you have the chance to tell them you love them that time still does not prepare you for their death. It doesn't mean that because you know their body is about to completely give out, that it would be any less painful.

I can remember the doctor telling my grandmother she only had 3-4 months to live. My mother was completely devastated. I, on the other hand, walked over to my grandmother and asked her what she wanted to do. I thought I had it all figured out in my head. We were going to rock out the time she had left and knowing she was preparing to make her transition; I would be okay when it happened. We went through the next few months, she even celebrated another birthday on December 7, 2012. By this time, she was very frail and couldn't really do anything for herself, but that didn't stop her from trying. We shared the same birthday month, so on my birthday December 31, 2012, I only had one wish. That wish was that she would dance with me. Every year since I was 13, my granny promised me a dance on my birthday. This year I didn't want it to be any different. She had no strength, but somewhere in her mind and body she mustered up enough to stand for 60 secs to dance with me. This would be the last dance and birthday she was physically here to celebrate with me. She passed away 7 days later, exactly one month after her 88th birthday. My mom and I had gotten dressed and was about to head to the hospital to see her when we got the call that she had peacefully passed at 7:33 AM. My heart sank, but I knew what I felt couldn't be worse than what my mother was feeling. I just wrapped my arms around her and hugged her for as long as she wanted to hold onto me. I must interject this. My grandmother's best friend, Claudia Everette, made a promise that she would take care of my grandmother. When we called her that morning, she told us she would meet us at the hospital before the funeral home came to get my granny. She arrived shortly after we did, walked over to my granny and kissed her several times. She asked a nurse to come help her and asked us if she could have the room for a little bit. We went outside for about 30 minutes.

When we came back to the room, my granny had gotten a bath, was dressed in silk leopard print pajamas with matching slippers. She had a purple scarf around her head, her jewelry placed on her and was wearing her favorite perfume. She looked so beautiful. When the guy from the funeral home arrived, he expressed that he had never seen anything like it before. That's true friendship.

My grandmother dying was rough, but again I didn't give myself the permission to grieve because I put my mother's grief before mine. I didn't think that what I felt was important, but it was. In the moment, I didn't feel like I had the right to be hurt. These are normal things that we often tell ourselves while on the cusp of an emotional wave. It's not fair to you or anyone you may encounter. Thinking that I had been prepared for her death was also a disservice emotionally. I was not prepared for the days and nights of longing for her. I wasn't even prepared to watch them close her casket. I stood there and when the Pastor handed me her glasses, I lost it. I broke down and couldn't believe it was real. I had given myself every pep talk. I had so many laughs with friends and family, but when the reality set in, I was a mess. The same with my siblings. I handled every aspect of their funerals from choosing the casket to my oldest brothers' clothes and colors. I wrote the obituaries for all three family members, newspaper announcements, etc. Everything I knew to do to keep my cool didn't work. Even in "preparing" for what I knew was ahead, I was not prepared. Give yourself some space to expect the unexpected. This is not easy. You can make every plan, think of every detail, you can go on with life even after their burial, but once your emotional wall gets weak and you start to feel, know that the thought of "I wasn't expecting this" or even questions of why will come. It doesn't matter if you know why, the fact that you were not prepared for life without your loved one is a real thing. You feel it and it hurts. We often seek or feel as though we need closure and most of the time we never get it. You must find that peace within yourself and know that you were loved and assure yourself that they know you loved them. Don't blame yourself for the things that happened that were out of your control. It is not your fault. The morning my baby brother was murdered, I had been by his house 3 times. For years after his death, I felt as though if I had stopped by one more time I could've saved him or jumped in front of the bullet. I felt like as much I as protected him all my life, this was the one time I wasn't there to do that. It took a lot of therapy and knowing that my brother would've felt worse if I had taken a bullet for him, for me to realize the plan of his life was out of my control. I realized that I could no longer blame myself for his murder. I know it doesn't feel good right now and you may still feel guilty but do the work to understand why it's not your fault. The end goal is to gain control over your life and learning how to live beyond your grief.

Preparation: Your story

_____

_____

_____

_____

_____

_____

_____

_____

_____

_____

_____

_____

Chapter 4

Feel How You Feel, No Apologies.

Don't tell me how to grieve!

Imagine going through the hardest time in your life and someone trying to dictate how you grieve? That's wild to even think of it happening, but it does. I can't count how many times I've heard, "It's been 5 years. You should be over it by now." Or you have those who tell you that you're strong and that you will be fine. That's very easy to say when that's not the seat one is currently sitting in. I knew I would okay, but I didn't see or know when that would happen. You know that you're strong, but some days you don't want to be and that's perfectly fine. As I previously stated, grief is not the same for everyone. You may express yourself in a different way but try to create some healthy habits. Grief can be tricky in the way of wanting to numb yourself from what you feel.

If you already have some underlying mental health issues, drinking or drug use issues, the urge to overindulge in those things may present itself. One thing I have realized is that grief is not limited to death. You can grieve the loss of a job, a relationship, a home or vehicle. There are many things that we grieve. Any emotions associated with grief can cause one to act or respond in unhealthy ways.

This is why it's important to go to therapy and to have a strong support system. Although you are entitled to feel however you want to feel, you don't want to bleed on people who did not cut you. You don't want to exhibit behaviors or put yourself in a position that can be harmful yourself or others. Grieving properly means taking complete responsibilities for yourself and those things you feel.

Take all the time you need to sort through what you feel and why you feel that way. All of it is important to your process. Do not let anyone put a time limit on your process. It's not something you can just get over, especially death. It doesn't matter if you "prepared" yourself or not. In my personal experience, I was in denial. I was hurt and extremely confused. I didn't display the emotions of someone who had just heard their sibling had been murdered. Be true to your process. Be angry, cry, be sad or any other way you feel. Just don't stay there. It is not easy. However, you will learn to live through it. You will be triggered, especially on holidays and birthdays, but you will get through it. Don't go to that event if you feel like you're not ready. Nobody has to be understanding, but you are entitled to give yourself that grace.

Sorting through your emotions

Chapter 5

Do Not Compare

We are not the same.

One of the biggest misconceptions about grief is that one person's pain is greater than the other. That one person's loss is greater than the other. None of this is true. I used to work for Verizon Wireless. I had a customer call in to disconnect her husband's phone because he had recently passed away. Amid the conversation, she began to cry. I tried to console her as best as I could and eventually, she regained the emotional strength to continue with the call. I will never forget what she said upon ending the call. She told me, "Grief is the price you pay for loving someone." I am not sure if those were her words, but they have stuck with me over the years.

Loving someone (no matter who it is) can be a painful experience when they leave this world. I know that my mother having to bury two of her three children and my father burying his only 2 boys, is a pain no parent wants to experience. As I said earlier, I always put my feelings on the back burner because I thought my pain couldn't compare to the hurt and pain they felt. It couldn't because the relationship wasn't the same.

However, that should never mean that what I feel is insignificant compared to theirs. You are broken, hurt, disgusted, confused, angry and lost. Those are just a few feelings. What you have experienced is yours to own. When talking to someone who is also grieving it can be taxing. What I mean by that is you find yourself explaining how you feel, and they return words seemingly trying to counter or top what you've just expressed. When that happens, I am sure you probably have or will shut down. Another thing that happens is you'll find yourself taking care of people emotionally, neglecting your own grief process. Speaking from my personal experience, this can create unhealthy habits for you. I took on this "I'm great" attitude. I only spoke on the loss of my people in a positive way. I had people tell me, "You are so strong. I don't see how you talk about them and not break down." My inside voice was always like, "You people won't let me break down, so what's the point?!" I laugh about it now because if people knew how many times I flipped them off in my head, they would've stopped saying it to me. In your process you must remember to be kind to yourself first. Do not compare what you feel to others and don't allow them to do it to you. It's okay to set boundaries related to how you grieve. You also must learn how to communicate differently when figuring out your process. This is a good place to give you an example of boundaries. How you communicate or how you allow others to communicate with you is essential. Not allowing someone to force their logic of how grief should look is a real thing, but it's not their grief they're trying to control, it's yours. No person has the right to dictate your process. No person has the right to compare their experience to yours. You will find that people can be insensitive, rude and very intrusive. Most people don't know they're being this way, but please understand you have the right to tell them about it. It doesn't matter if it's a family member, friend or stranger; you have to be in control of how you grieve. It's your journey. It's your process. It's just as much your loss than it is anyone else who loved that person.

Connecting with people (i.e family, friends or a new human) over grief can be a good thing, but I strongly suggest that you find a therapist that will help you properly place and work through your emotions. There is lots of trauma that comes with grief from the aspect of unanswered questions, unforgiveness and how a person leaves this earth. There is so much work to do because grief will always be a part of your time. There's a quote that I absolutely hate that says, "Time heals all wounds". That is not true! Time, proper therapy, self-care, and support helps you to understand the stages of grief as it applies to your life. The pain, although bearable some days, will never go away. It's been over 12 years since losing both my brothers and my grandparents. Some days I am laughing and smiling at the thought of them, but when I find myself in that rabbit hole of thoughts, the pain is as if they died yesterday. However, knowing my triggers, knowing what I feel and expressing that via therapy or a journal, I can work my way out of that hole and back into life. It can be depressing but you are not alone. Feel how you feel, but don't stay there. Get up, Go out and LIVE. You will have great days. Days filled with laughter, memories of what was and creating new memories with your loved ones in mind. Then, you will have days where you feel like you're living in the freshest moment of their passing. You will relive the day(s). You will feel the pain and the tears will cloud your vision. It is in those times that you allow yourself to feel it, discover new emotions and forge forward with a better understanding of that wave. You may not feel like you won't survive, but you will. Grief is a lifelong journey filled with unexpected twist and turns. Like the ocean, at times the waves can be gentle. Other times they can be so strong that it feels like you're going to be swept away. No matter which way it goes, you will find your

way and be better because you did it your way.

RESOURCES:

betterhelp.com

talkspace.com

SUICIDE HOTLINE

Dial 988 to speak with someone

DRUG AND ALCOHOL HELPLINE:

SAMHSA 1-800-662-(HELP) 4357

Setting Boundaries

Dearly Beloved (The Cost of Love)

By Zipporiah S. Brockman

I'm sure you're assuming this is a lovely read on marriage and all the wonderful things that come with it. Let me assure you, it's not. Talking about those you've loved while they were here on earth is such a beautiful thing, but what about when they die? The conversation takes so many turns that you don't quite know exactly what to say. While your emotions drive your feelings, you search frantically to find a common place to settle in your mind about everything going on in your body. From their presence, then their absence and the heartbreaking realization that they are never coming back. When I was growing up, all we had were photos to shuffle through for a few hours to satisfy our feelings, then put that box away and not look back for quite some time.

Now we have cell phones, computers and tablets that eternally memorialize our loved ones. We become so attached to those photos, videos, voice memos or messages that we unintentionally create a virtual cemetery for them. I don't know how many times I've scrolled across photos of my brothers, my grandmother, pawpaw and my best friend and just broke down crying for hours on end. I promised myself many times that I would delete the photos because the memories I have in my heart would do just fine, but then when it came time to remove them, I felt like I was wrong to even have considered it. I felt like maybe I would somehow forget about them or that they may feel like I'm erasing them in a way. I mean…what the heck is that, really? I've thought to myself," Am I weird or what's wrong with me?"

I've often had a sense that all of those mentioned above were somehow following me or screwing with me in their own way since they've passed, but seriously, what can they do to me when they're dead?! Why am I paying for extra storage to house 5.6 GB of photos, videos and messages that don't really hold a candle to the memories in my head and heart.

It's crippling to think of going through my phone, even scrolling through my social media page or commenting on their pages just to say "I miss you" when I know just saying those words into the wind will carry the message directly to them. Maybe I'm just a creep like that, but I stand up for all the creeps who just can't seem to detach themselves from the things or the idea of what "moving on" is supposed to look like. For however long we had our loved ones, the fact is they are physically not here. We each, in whatever way makes us comfortable and keeps us as close to sanity as possible, have partially accepted that fact, but the pain of completely letting go of those photos, that sweater, hat, notebook, cologne, busted pair of shoes, for some we are just not ready to take it on.

So, dearly beloved, although we were not granted all the time we would've liked with you, we live our lives day after day with you in our hearts. Each new chapter that we begin without you is another opportunity to share a piece of you with the world. For as long as it takes you will continue to take up space in our phones, tablets, our social media and most certainly in our hearts.

Made in the USA
Middletown, DE
06 February 2025